WHAT IT MEANS TO BE

SERIES

PUBLISHER	Joseph R. DeVarennes
PUBLICATION DIRECTOR	Kenneth H. Pearson
ADVISORS	Roger Aubin Robert Furlonger
PROJECT CO-ORDINATOR	Sarah Swartz
EDITORIAL MANAGER	Jocelyn Smyth
EDITORS	Ann Martin Shelley McGuinness Robin Rivers Mayta Tannenbaum
PRODUCTION MANAGER	Ernest Homewood
PRODUCTION ASSISTANTS	Kathy Kishimoto Douglas Parker
PUBLICATION ADMINISTRATOR	Clare Adam

Canadian Cataloguing in Publication Data

Schemenauer, Elma
  A friend

(What it means to be; v. 1)
ISBN 0-7172-2225-X

1. Friendship — Juvenile literature.
I. Title.   II. Series.

BJ1533.F8S34 1987   j158'.24   C86-095057-3

WHAT IT MEANS TO BE...

A FRIEND

Written by
Elma Schemenauer

Illustrated by
Steve Pileggi

A friend plays with you.

Tammy and Mitchell ran across the lawn. They were playing shadow tag. "I stepped on your shadow, so you're IT!" shouted Mitchell.

Then it was Tammy's turn to step on Mitchell's shadow. She chased him around the apple tree. Faster and faster she ran.

Tammy and Mitchell live next door to each other. They play together a lot. Mitchell and Tammy are friends.

You can play tag and lots of other games with a friend. Taking turns with your friend is fun. Being a good sport is part of being a friend.

A friend likes many of the same things you like.

"Watch me. I'm a bird!" called Hannah. She flapped her arms as she whooshed down the slide in the school playground.

"I'm a spaceship," yelled Janice. "Look out! I'm coming in for a landing." She whooshed down the slide.

Soon it was snack time. Hannah and Janice sat together. They both liked raisins. So Hannah gave Janice some of her raisins.

Hannah and Janice both like playing on the slide and eating raisins. They like a lot of the same things. Janice and Hannah are friends.

You probably like many of the things your friends enjoy. That's one reason you became friends in the first place.

A friend helps you when you need help.

Vroom! Vroom! Vroom! Jason and Bobby were playing with their trucks. Suddenly a big boy came along and kicked sand at Bobby. He grabbed Bobby's best green truck. Then the big boy threw the truck into the bushes and ran away laughing.

"Don't cry, Bobby," said Jason, patting Bobby on the back. He brushed the sand off Bobby. Then Jason helped Bobby find the truck.

Jason and Bobby help each other. They are nice to each other. Jason and Bobby are friends.

Being friends means helping each other. What do you do when your friend is hurt, or has lost something, or is having trouble getting a job done? If you are a friend, you do whatever you can to help.

A friend cares what happens to you.

Mitchell and Tammy were climbing the apple tree
in front of Tammy's house. "Higher! Go up
higher, Mitchell," shouted Tammy. "Let's climb
up and get those big red apples at the top."

Mitchell looked unhappy. "Your mom said
we're not supposed to climb any higher than this
branch with the birdhouse on it."

"Well, I'm going up anyway," said Tammy.
"Get out of my way, Mitchell!"

"No, Tammy!" yelled Mitchell. "You might
fall and break your leg."

Tammy scrambled past Mitchell and onto a higher branch of the apple tree. Then she climbed onto an even higher branch.

"I'm going to tell your mom, Tammy," said Mitchell, starting to climb down the tree.

Tammy stopped. "If you tell, then you're not my friend any more, Mitchell."

"Oh, yes, he is," said Tammy's mom, coming out of the house to get the mail. "Tammy, you come down this instant. You should be glad you have a friend like Mitchell. He wants to keep you from getting hurt."

Sometimes your friends have very good reasons for disagreeing with you. Friends shouldn't tell on each other just to get attention or to cause trouble. But if a situation is dangerous or if you have a problem that is too big for you to solve yourself, you should ask an adult to help.

A friend treats you fairly.

Ding! Ding! The ice cream truck was coming. Paul looked for his money. He finally found it and ran out to the street corner.

By the time Paul got there, lots of kids were already lined up for ice cream. Paul pushed in ahead of his friend Jason. "I have to go in front of you, Jason," he said. "My brother's waiting for me to go play soccer."

"That's not fair, Paul," said Colette, who was now in line behind them. "Jason was here before you were!"

Paul was so busy thinking about himself and his own plans that he pushed ahead of his friend.

"I'm in a hurry too, Paul," said Jason, looking his friend straight in the eye. "My big brother's waiting to take me to the park."

"But I couldn't find my money," said Paul. "If I had, I would have been here before you."

"Aw, come on Paul. Be fair," said Colette. "You wouldn't want me pushing into line ahead of you, would you?"

Paul thought for a moment. "No, I guess not. I'm sorry, Jason," he said slowly.

By this time Paul and Jason were at the door of the ice cream truck. Paul stepped back to let his friend go first.

Being fair is part of being a friend. Sometimes you can be so busy thinking about yourself, you may forget about your friend. If you make this mistake, try to think of a way to fix things up again. Remember that other people are just as important as you are.

A friend shares things with you.

Mitchell was crying. On the way to the ice cream truck, he'd lost his money. Now he didn't have enough money for ice cream.

"What kind do you like best, Mitch?" asked his friend Tammy.

"Chocolate," said Mitchell through his tears.

Tammy had just enough money for one treat. When it was her turn, she bought a chocolate ice cream bar. She carefully broke it in half. Then she gave half to Mitchell. The ice cream tasted delicious.

You and your friends share your toys. You share your pencils and paper. And when you share a special treat, like an ice cream bar, it seems to taste better than if you ate the whole thing yourself.

A friend shares thoughts and feelings with you.

One day Colette was sad when she came to school. "I feel lonesome," she said. "My mom and dad have gone on a trip. They'll be gone a long time."

"I'm sorry you feel lonesome," said Kim. "I know how you feel. Last summer when my mom went into the hospital, I was lonesome too."

Kim thought for a moment. "Maybe we could write your mom and dad a letter, Colette," she suggested.

Friends share both happy and sad feelings with each other. When a friend feels sad, you should let your friend know you are sorry. Try to think of ways to help your friend feel better.

Sometimes even good friends fight.

Hannah and Janice were taking their dolls for a walk. Just for fun, Hannah pushed Janice off the sidewalk. Just for fun, Janice pushed Hannah.

Then Hannah pushed Janice, and Janice pushed Hannah, and soon Hannah got angry. "You look stupid, Janice," she said. "Your doll is stupid too."

Janice started to cry. She grabbed Hannah's doll and threw it down in the mud. The doll's pretty yellow coat got all dirty. "You're not my friend any more!" screamed Hannah. Both girls grabbed their dolls and ran home crying.

Fooling around can be fun, but only as long as your friend thinks it's fun too. If your friend starts feeling sad or angry, it is time to stop.

After a fight, you can become friends again.

"You should tell Hannah you're sorry you threw her doll in the mud," said Janice's mom when Janice came home.

"I don't want to," cried Janice.

But a few days later, Janice started to feel lonesome for Hannah. She went over and rang Hannah's doorbell. "Can you come out to play?" she asked. "I'm sorry your doll got dirty."

"I'm sorry I called you stupid," said Hannah. "Let's go to the playground."

"Okay, but no pushing," said Janice.

"Right. No pushing," said Hannah.

If you say "I'm sorry," you can usually become friends again. It's a good idea to talk about what made you and your friend fight. It's also good to think about how you can keep from fighting again.

A friend feels happy when you are happy.

"Hurrah! I'm going to be in a parade!" shouted Colette. "My mom's going to help me make a costume. I'm going to have a big flag to carry. And I'm going to play my accordion. There'll be prizes and everything!"

Kim wished she could be in the parade too. But she also wanted her friend to have a good time. "I hope you win a prize," she said. "I know you're a good accordion player."

Kim thought for a moment. Then she said, "I could ask my dad to let you ride in the soapbox car he made for me. You could even tie your flag to it."

"Oh, Kim. That would be great!" said Colette. Her eyes were shining.

If you are a friend, you will feel happy and excited when your friend is happy. You will remember that exciting things happen to you too.

Friends trust each other.

It was already suppertime, and Colette hadn't brought Kim's soapbox car back from the parade.

"I just hope she didn't break the soapbox car," said Kim's dad. "I put a lot of work into making it."

"Oh, I know Colette is taking good care of it," said Kim. "She's my friend and I trust her."

Sure enough, just after dinner, Colette was at Kim's door. "Sorry I'm late," said Colette. "Mom and I took my grandpa home after the parade. That's why I wasn't here sooner. Here's your soapbox car, Kim, safe and sound."

You trust your friends, and you want your friends to trust you too. If you are a good friend, people can trust you to take care of their things. They can also trust you to keep your promises.

Friends appreciate what you do for them.

Jason was sick in bed. His friend Bobby brought over a game to play. But Jason was so busy reading his comic book that he hardly noticed Bobby.

Bobby's game was about zoo animals. He showed the pieces to Jason. There was a fierce-looking lion and a hump-backed camel. There was also a crocodile with its mouth wide open.

"I don't care about animals right now," said Jason crossly. "I'm interested in space. I'm reading about space monsters!"

Bobby felt sad. He left the game on Jason's bed and went home.

For three days Bobby stayed away from Jason's house. At last Jason phoned. "Why don't you come and see me? I'm still sick, you know."

"You didn't play with me last time I was there," said Bobby in a grumpy voice.

"I'm sorry," said Jason. "Hey, thanks for that game you brought. I played it with my mom. It's really great. Why don't you come and play it with me?"

When someone does something nice for you, it's best to show your appreciation and say thank you right away. If you forget and act as though you don't care, you will probably make your friend unhappy. In that case, be sure to say thank you as soon as you remember.

A friend shows you new things.

Ryan was new at school. At first he felt sad and lonely because he didn't have any friends yet. One day Ryan's parents let him bring his robot to school.

"Look at Ryan's robot!" said Kim. "It's almost as big as I am."

"Come sit with me, Ryan," said Paul. "I want to see your robot. Look at the light on top of your robot's head. What's the light for?"

Ryan knew a lot about robots. He made his robot walk and talk. He explained what the robot was made of and what the light was for. He showed all the kids how the robot worked.

Showing something interesting or exciting can be a good way to make new friends. If people see you want to share with them, they will know you will be a good friend.

A real friend likes you for yourself.

The next day Ryan didn't bring his robot with him.

As the kids were getting on the school bus to go home, Ryan saw an empty seat beside Paul. "Can I sit with you?" he asked.

"No, I don't want you to sit here, Ryan," said Paul.

When Ryan had the robot, Paul wanted to be his friend. But when Ryan didn't have his robot, Paul didn't act friendly.

Just then Kim got on the bus. "Come sit with me, Ryan," she called. "I'm playing hockey tomorrow. Can you come too?"

Real friends like you because of who you are, not because of what you have. Real friends don't care if you have a lot of toys or a few toys. They like you because you're you!

It's fun to make new friends.

"Way to go, Ryan!" yelled Kim, skating past him. "That was a good pass. You're learning fast."

"Hey, Ryan," said Bobby after hockey practice. "Maybe you could come to my house tomorrow. Ask your mom."

Before long, Ryan was friends with lots of kids from the hockey team—like Kim and Bobby. Soon he started making friends with Jason and Colette.

When new kids move into your neighborhood, they often don't have anyone to play with. You can be friendly by asking them to join your games. You can help them make new friends, and you can make new friends too.

There is always room for another friend.

"Quick! Get into the spaceship," yelled Bobby.
"We're space police. We're catching space
pirates." Bobby and Paul ran towards a big
cardboard box. They had made it into a
spaceship.

Just then Ryan came along. "Can I ride in the
spaceship too? I can be your navigator."

"He's right," said Bobby. "He can help us find
our way. Let's take him along."

"Okay, Ryan," said Paul, "You can be our
navigator for today. Get in."

"5-4-3-2-1 . . . BLASTOFF!" shouted Ryan.

Even though you may enjoy playing with one special
friend, you can play with other kids too. You can
have many friends.

Friends are important.

It was Ryan's birthday. Ryan's mom brought a birthday cake to school for Ryan to share with his new friends. How happy Ryan felt! "I didn't like this school at first," he said. "Now I love it because I have lots of friends,"

"Happy birthday to you," sang Ryan's friends.

You don't need a lot of friends to be happy, but everybody needs some friends. Here are some things you can do to help you make and keep friends.

- Share with others.
- Listen to others.
- Take turns and be a good sport.
- Help others.

Printed and Bound in the United States of America